The Mother's Day Book

Rita Storey

W
FRANKLIN WATTS
LONDON•SYDNEY

Franklin Watts
First published in Great Britain in 2015 by
The Watts Publishing Group

Credits
Editor: Sarah Ridley
Design: Storeybooks
Cover design: Cathryn Gilbert
Photography Tudor Photography, Banbury unless
   otherwise stated

Dewey number 394.2628
HB ISBN 978 1 4451 3976 0
Library ebook ISBN 978 1 4451 3880 0

Printed in China

Picture credits:
Borders and backgrounds; **Polina Katritch/Shutterstock,
ARaspopova/Shutterstock, Mikhaylova Liubov/
Shutterstock;** Flowers in heading; **gst/Shutterstock,
Bird Ann Precious/Shutterstock;** Notebook; **Garsya/
Shutterstock; Anibal Trejo/Shutterstock p4; Madlen/
Shutterstock p5t; MAHATHIR MOHD YASIN/Shutterstock
p5bl; Mat Hayward/Shutterstock p5bm; 1nana1/
Shutterstock p5br;** Wikimedia Commons/Northern
pacific Railway p7br; FPG/Getty Images p10; Linda
Macpherson/Shutterstock p21; Annareichel/Shutterstock
pp24/25; Wikimedia Commons/By Evert Odekerken
p28t; Wikimedia Commons p28m; Wikimedia
Commons p28b.

MIX
Paper from
responsible sources
FSC® C104740
FSC
www.fsc.org

Franklin Watts
An imprint of Hachette Children's Group
Part of The Watts Publishing Group
Carmelite House
50 Victoria Embankment
London EC4Y 0DZ

An Hachette UK Company
www.hachette.co.uk

www.franklinwatts.co.uk

Contents

What is Mother's Day?

Mother's Day is the day when children say thank you to their mother for all she has done for them. In the United Kingdom it is celebrated on the fourth Sunday in Lent and in the United States of America, Australia and New Zealand it is celebrated on the second Sunday in May.

Ancient spring festivals

Both the ancient Greeks and the ancient Romans celebrated spring festivals held in honour of the 'Mother of the Gods'. The Greeks celebrated two goddesses – Gaia the goddess of the Earth and her daughter Rhea, and the Romans honoured the goddess Cybele.

This statue forms part of the Fountain of Cibeles (Cybele) in Madrid, Spain.

Mothering Sunday

In the United Kingdom, Mother's Day is also known as Mothering Sunday. In the Middle Ages (1154–1485), Mothering Sunday was a day when people visited their 'Mother Church', the main church or cathedral in the area. The day was also known as Refreshment Sunday. This is because the Church allowed people to relax the rules of the forty days of fasting during Lent in order to allow families to enjoy a meal together.

A rare day off

In the 18th and 19th centuries children and young people who were working away from home as servants or apprentices sometimes only had one day off a year, on Mothering Sunday. As they walked home, many of them picked a bunch of wild flowers to take home to their mother as a gift.

Mother's Day

By the 1900s fewer people were celebrating Mothering Sunday. But then a revival began.

In the United States of America, Anna Jarvis (see pages 10–11) campaigned for a special day to honour mothers and, in 1914, the US government gave their support to the idea. The idea was taken up by some people in the United Kingdom, who set about persuading people to celebrate Mothering Sunday again.

Then, during the Second World War (1939–45), people saw that American troops, who were stationed in Britain, were celebrating Mother's Day by sending gifts and cards. British people started to do the same but on Mothering Sunday, rather than in May. Today Mother's Day is celebrated in many countries around the world.

Cards

Handmade Mother's Day cards are often kept and treasured. They are so much nicer to receive than shop bought ones.

You will need:
- A4 sheet of stiff yellow paper
- scissors • ruler and pencil
- sticky tape
- red and blue poster paint • baking tray
- scrap of card
- A4 sheet of thin white card

I love you this much

1. Cut the yellow paper into three long strips, 7cm wide. Join the strips together using sticky tape in order to make one long strip.

2. Starting at one end, fold over the first 4cm of the long paper strip. Turn the paper strip over and fold the next 4cm. Keep turning over and folding to make a zig-zag shape (see right).

3. Squeeze a blob of red paint onto a baking tray. Spread it out with the scrap of card. Press your left hand into it. Make a handprint on the thin white card. Wash your hands. Repeat using blue paint to make a print of your right hand. Cut out the prints. Tape them onto each end of the folded paper strip.

4. Write your message on the folded card.

I love you this much

Flower bouquet

1 Fold one sheet of the blue card in half. Use the pencil and ruler to make two marks, 3.5cm apart, along the central fold. Make two cuts, 2.5cm long. Open out the card.

2 Use the templates on page 30 to trace and cut out coloured paper shapes.

3 Glue the paper flowers onto the oval part of the green paper shape. Leave to dry. Open up the card and glue the paper bouquet onto the front of the fold.

4 Write your message inside the card.

Happy Mother's Day

Mother's Day cards

Since its beginnings in the United States of America in 1908, making or buying a card for Mother's Day has been the most popular way to say a big 'thank you' to mums.

Millions of printed Mother's Day cards are sent every year. Many children choose to make their own cards instead of buying one. Then they can include a special message or picture for their mother.

In Honor of the Best Mother who ever lived Your Mother

Designed by Northern Pacific Railways in the USA in 1916, this postcard was one of the first printed Mother's Day cards.

Sweet treats

These homemade sweets make a lovely Mother's Day gift. Place them in a clear bag tied up with a pretty ribbon.

You will need:

- 300g chocolate buttons
- 3 tablespoons golden syrup
- 125g butter
- bowl • saucepan filled with hot water
- spoon • 100g mini marshmallows
- 200g digestive biscuits
- 2 x see-through bags
- rolling pin • pastry board
- fish slice
- 30cm ribbon

Mini rocky road

1 Put the chocolate buttons, golden syrup and butter in a bowl. Ask an adult to melt them over a pan of hot water.

2 Add the marshmallows to the melted mixture.

3 Put the biscuits into a plastic bag. Use the rolling pin to break them up. Empty the biscuit pieces into the bowl and mix everything together.

4 Put small heaps of the mixture onto the pastry board and place them in the fridge for two hours or until completely set. Use a fish slice to take them off the board. Put them into a see-through bag and tie it closed with a pretty ribbon.

Chocolate peppermint creams

1. Place both blocks of icing on the board and knead the peppermint oil into them. Roll out the icing and use the biscuit cutter to cut out the peppermint creams.

2. Ask an adult to melt the dark chocolate in a bowl over a pan of hot water. Ask them to melt the white chocolate in a separate bowl.

3. Hold a peppermint cream by one edge and dip it carefully into either the dark or milk chocolate up to the middle. Place on a rack to dry. Repeat with the remaining peppermint creams.

4. When the chocolate has set, place the peppermint creams in a gift bag. Tie up the bag with a pretty ribbon.

You will need:

- 2 x 125g blocks of fondant icing (one coloured green using food colouring)
- pastry board, dusted with icing sugar
- few drops peppermint oil
- rolling pin
- small biscuit cutter
- 100g each of dark and white chocolate, broken into pieces
- 2 bowls
- saucepan filled with hot water
- cooling rack
- see-through gift bag and ribbon

Make a gift tag by folding a rectangle of card (10cm x 5cm) in half. Make a hole in the corner with a hole punch. Thread a ribbon through.

Happy Mother's Day

When working children went home to visit their mothers on Mothering Sunday (see page 5) they would often pick a posy of wild flowers to take back as a present. We still carry on the tradition today. Flowers and sweets are the most popular Mother's Day gifts but today most of us buy these gifts. Chocolate manufacturers, card manufacturers and retailers, supermarkets, restaurant owners and florists all make a lot of money on Mother's Day.

Mother's Day today

Mother's Day in the USA

The Mother's Day traditions that we celebrate today come from the United States of America. Julia Ward Howe (see page 28) suggested that there should be a mother's day for peace in 1870 but it was Anna Jarvis who established Mother's Day as we know it.

Anna Jarvis (1864–1948)

When Anna Jarvis' mother died in 1905, Anna decided to persuade people in her mother's home town of Webster, West Virginia, to hold a church service in honour of her mother and the work of all mothers. The first Mother's Day was celebrated on 10 May 1908 and the idea became so popular that in 1914, US President Woodrow Wilson made the second Sunday in May the official Mother's Day.

Soon Mother's Day became a time when shops made a lot of money from selling gifts, flowers and cards. Anna Jarvis was so disappointed by this that she spent many years of her life trying to persuade people to return to her original idea of simply spending time with your mother on Mother's Day to thank her for everything she does.

Special flowers

On the first official Mother's Day in 1908, Anna Jarvis could not attend the church service in Webster, West Virginia, because she was at another event in Philadelphia. However, she sent 500 white carnations for the Webster church congregation to wear. The white carnation was her mother's favourite flower and a symbol of peace and purity.

In the years that followed, wearing a white carnation on Mother's Day became so popular that florists ran out days in advance. Over time, people began to wear a red carnation for a mother who was still alive and a white one if their mother had died. Some mothers also wore yellow carnations to remember children who had died.

Mother's Day around the world

AUSTRALIA, NEW ZEALAND, CANADA AND THE UNITED STATES OF AMERICA – second Sunday in May. Celebrated by wearing carnations and giving cards and gifts.

BRAZIL – second Sunday in May. An important celebration with church services, children's shows and barbeques.

MEXICO – 10 May. Celebrated by church services at which an early morning meal is given to all mothers.

FRANCE – last Sunday in May. Children give their mother small gifts and a card. Traditionally the mother is given a cake in the shape of a bouquet of flowers.

THAILAND – 12 August. Many Thai children kneel at the feet of their mother in a ceremony where they honour her for all she has done for them. The date of Mother's Day is the birthday of Queen Sirikit, who is seen as mother to all Thai people.

Breakfast

It is traditional to spoil your mother on Mother's Day. This yummy breakfast would be a great start to her day.

You will need:
- pretty wine glass
- tub of natural yoghurt
- tablespoon
- fruit (blueberries, strawberries – chopped up if large)
- granola or muesli

Yoghurt parfait

1 Put a spoonful of yoghurt into the bottom of the glass.

2 Add a layer of fruit.

3 Add another spoonful of yoghurt.

4 Spinkle a layer of granola or muesli.

5 Finish with another layer of yoghurt and some fruit to decorate.

Tips for making breakfast
- Do not try cooking anything too complicated. These recipes are easy but cereal and fruit will look just as good. Lay the table or a tray, adding your card and a small bunch of flowers.
- Your mum may want to lie in bed for a little longer on Mother's Day so do not start making breakfast too early. You could serve brunch instead.

Remember to do the washing up as well!

Cinnamon bagels

1 Put a dessertspoon of sugar and the cinnamon into the bag. Hold the bag closed and shake it to mix the sugar and cinnamon together.

2 Ask an adult to split the bagel in half. Toast the bagel in a toaster (or ask an adult to grill it).

3 Put it on a plate and spread with butter. Sprinkle on the cinnamon sugar.

You will need:
- dessertspoon of sugar
- quarter teaspoon of cinnamon
- small plastic bag
- a plain bagel
- sharp knife
- butter
- plate

Pizza bagels

1 Ask an adult to split the bagel in half. Toast the bagel in a toaster (or ask an adult to grill it). Spread each cut side with butter.

2 Add some tomato pizza sauce, some chopped ham and a layer of grated cheese.

3 Ask an adult to put the pizza bagels under a grill for a few minutes until the cheese has melted.

You will need:
- a bagel
- sharp knife
- butter
- plate
- tomato pizza sauce
- chopped ham
- grated cheese

13

Presents

Homemade gifts will mean much more to your mum than anything you could buy from the shops. These presents will be a reminder of your love long after Mother's Day is over.

You will need:

- cling film
- 500g air-dry clay
- rolling pin
- pencil or pen
- blunt knife
- small bowl
- acrylic craft paint and paintbrush
- PVA glue

Hand-shaped ring bowl

1. Lay some cling film on a work surface. Roll out the clay on the cling film with the rolling pin until it is larger than your hand.

2. Press one hand into the clay. Draw around your hand with a pencil or an old ballpoint pen.

3. Lift up your hand and use a blunt knife to cut around the shape.

4. Lay the cling film with the clay hand shape on it in a bowl. Leave it to dry overnight.

5. Lift the hand-shaped clay bowl off the cling film. Paint the inside of the bowl with acrylic craft paint. Leave to dry. Turn it over and paint the other side. Leave to dry.

6. Repeat step 5 using PVA glue to varnish your bowl. Your mum can use the bowl to keep her rings safe.

Bookmark

1 Ask someone to take a picture of you, posing like the girl in the photo.

2 Ask an adult to help you size your photo so that it is 6cm at its widest point. Print it out and cut it out.

3 Decorate the card with felt-tip pens.

4 Tape the photo to the top of the decorated card.

Promise box

1 Cover the box in spotty wrapping paper. Cut out an oval from the white paper. Glue it onto the front of the box. Cut out a few butterflies from the wrapping paper. Glue them onto the box as shown in the picture. Write 'Promise Box' on the white oval.

2 Write a promise onto each slip of paper. Here are some ideas:
I promise to wash up on Mondays;
I promise to make my bed.
Post the promise slips inside the decorated box. Your mum can use your promises when she needs them.

Promise Box

Present cards

A homemade card is always very special to any mother. The cards on these two pages contain a thoughtful Mother's Day gift too.

Handbag card

1   Cut the end off the box. Cover the outside of the box with tape.

2   Trace and cut out the handbag template on page 29 and use it to cut out a blue card handbag. Use the handbag flap template to cut a flap from the blue spotty paper. Glue it onto the card handbag, as shown.

3   Use the bow templates on page 29 to cut out two paper bows. Glue the bow base onto the flap, as shown. Fold the ends of the bow into the middle and glue them in the centre of the bow base. Cut a strip of spotty paper. Glue it across the bottom of the card. Write 'Happy Mother's Day' above the paper strip.

4   With the base of the box level with the bottom edge of the card handbag, tape the box onto the centre, at the back. Fill the box with small gifts so that they can be seen from the front.

Happy Mother's Day

Teacup card

1. Cut the end off the box. Cover the outside of the box with tape.

2. Trace and cut out the teacup template on page 29 and use it to draw a teacup shape on the purple card. Glue on the blue and yellow strips of card as shown. Trim them to fit.

3. Cut out the card teacup.

4. With the base of the box level with the bottom edge, tape the box onto the back of the card teacup as shown. Fill the box with small gifts so that they can be seen from the front. Write your message on the gift card. Tape the gift card's ribbon to the inside of the teacup card.

You will need:
- small cardboard box
- white tape
- pencil and thin white paper (for tracing the template)
- scissors
- A4 sheet thin purple card
- 1cm x 26cm strips of thin blue and yellow card
- glue and spreader
- sticky tape
- small presents such as cookies and wrapped tea bags
- gift card and ribbon
- sticky tape

Coffee mug card

1. To make the coffee mug card use red card and the template on page 30. Follow the instructions for the teacup card above. Decorate the mug with spots cut from white paper. Write your message on the card.

2. Fill the box with wrapped muffins or cookies and a small bag of fresh coffee.

Happy Mother's Day

Mother tree

Mother's Day is a good time to find out about **all** the mothers in your family. Do you know when your grandmother or her mother (your great-grandmother) were born? Find out as much as you can about them and display all the facts on a 'mother tree'.

You will need:
- pencil
- A3 sheet of stiff white paper
- green paint • brown paint
- paintbrush
- pencil and thin white paper (for tracing the template)
- scissors • A4 sheet thin green paper
- glue and spreader

1 Paint the shape of a tree on the white paper. Leave to dry.

2 Paint on the branches and tree trunk as shown in the picture. Leave to dry.

3 Trace the template on page 30 and use it to cut six folded leaf shapes from thin green paper.

4 Ask your mum the questions listed on page 19. Write the answers inside the leaves. Glue them onto the tree.

5   Repeat step 4 for your dad, stepdad or mother's partner.

6   Ask if there are any photographs of any of the mothers on your mother tree. If so, photocopy them to stick onto the front of the leaves.

Do the people in the photographs look alike?

great-grandma

grandma

Questions to ask your mum

What was your surname when you were born? (This is called a maiden name as some people change their surname when they get married.)

When were you born?

What was your mother's maiden name?

When was she born?

What were your grandmothers' maiden names? (Remember to ask about both of your great-grandmothers.)

When were they born?

If you want to add more information, you could also gather information about where they were all born and add it to your leaves.

Father's Day is in June. You could follow these instructions to make your dad a father tree.

Lots of different mothers

There are lots of different types of mothers who love and care for children. A birth mother is the mother who gave birth to you. If you are adopted, your mother will love and care for you but she did not give birth to you. A foster mother loves and cares for children whose mothers are not able to do so. A stepmother is the wife of your father if your parents have split up. Mother's Day celebrates all mothers.

Cupcake posy

In the past, children often brought gifts of a posy of flowers and a Simnel cake when they visited home on Mothering Sunday. These cupcakes combine both of these gift ideas.

You will need:

- fondant icing
- yellow, pink, purple, red, blue and green food colouring
- rolling pin
- 6 plain cupcakes
- green buttercream (see below)
- knife • 6 jelly sweets
- painted flowerpot
- polystyrene ball
- 6 cocktail sticks

1   Divide the block of fondant icing into six balls. Knead 3 drops of yellow food colouring into one ball. Now divide the yellow icing into five small balls and roll them out to form circles of icing.

2   Pinch the edge of each circle to make a petal shape.

Buttercream
140g soft butter
280g sieved icing sugar
1 tablespoon of milk
2 drops of vanilla essence
3 drops of green food colouring
Beat everything together in a bowl until it is smooth.

3   Use the knife to spread green buttercream over the top of a cupcake.

4   Press five icing petals onto the buttercream with the pinched points joining in the middle. Press a jelly sweet into the centre.

5 Repeat steps 1–4 with pink, red, blue, purple and yellow icing petals to decorate the other five cupcakes.

6 Push the polystyrene ball into the bottom of the flowerpot. Push a cocktail stick into the middle of the ball. Push five more cocktail sticks into the ball, spacing them out equally.

4 Press the base of each cupcake onto the sticks to make a posy of cupcakes.

Simnel cake

Simnel cake is a fruit cake which has a layer of marzipan baked into the middle. It is decorated with another layer of marzipan and 11 marzipan balls. The 11 marzipan balls represent 11 of Jesus' disciples (minus Judas, the disciple who betrayed Jesus).

At first this cake was linked to Mothering Sunday. Girls who worked as servants in big houses were often allowed to bake a Simnel cake as a gift to take to their mothers. Today it is more usual to bake a Simnel cake for Easter Sunday.

Indoor herb garden

A gift of an indoor garden of herbs or flowers is a fragrant and colourful gift for Mother's Day.

You will need:
- three small empty coffee/cocoa/syrup cans (the type with lids)
- acrylic craft paint
- paintbrush • scissors
- pencil and thin white paper (for tracing the template)
- sheet of: pink, green and yellow paper
- small stones • compost
- trowel • PVA glue
- three small herb plants

1 Ask an adult to make some holes in the bottom of the cans. Paint the outside of the cans. Leave to dry.

2 Use the thin white paper to trace the templates on page 30 and cut out six large circles and six small circles from the coloured paper.

3 Glue a small paper circle onto the centre of a large paper circle of a different colour. Glue the circles onto the tins.

4 Put a layer of small stones into the bottom of each can. Use the trowel to add some compost on top of the stones.

5 Paint a layer of PVA glue over the outside of each can to stop the decoration peeling off when you water the plants.

22

6 Plant a different herb plant in each pot. Fill up with compost. Press the compost gently to firm the plant in place. Water the plants.

When the plants get too big for the pots, plant them in a sunny spot in the garden.

Herbs to plant

Mint – quick to grow. Very nice with lamb.

Parsley – good chopped into omelettes or scrambled eggs.

Basil – easy to grow. Great in tomato sauce on pasta or pizza.

Chives – give an onion flavour which is good in omelettes and scrambled eggs.

thyme

mint

Parsley

Indoor flowers

Follow step 1 on page 22. Use a larger can such as a clean paint can. Follow step 4 on page 22. Plant a begonia bulb in the can. Cover the bulb with a layer of compost 1cm deep. Water the pot and place it on a sunny windowsill.

The bulb will begin to grow and give a lovely display of flowers in the early summer.

Sun Mother

An indigenous Australian creation story

At the very beginning of time, when Earth was a barren rock, the Father of the Spirits awoke the Sun Mother who was sleeping in the darkness. As she awoke, warm sunlight spread out from her and lit up everything around her.

The Father of the Spirits said that it was time for her to go down to Earth and wake up all of the Earth spirits. The Sun Mother did as she was asked. As she woke, the spirits, flowers, trees and plants of every description began to grow and flourish.

When she returned, the Father of the Spirits was pleased but he asked her to visit Earth again and this time he asked her to wake the spirits of the caves and dark places. Sun Mother went back down to Earth and this time she flooded the caves and dark places with her light. As she did so millions of insects flew from the caves and populated Earth.

Sun Mother once more returned to the Father of the Spirits but once again he asked her to return to Earth. This time she used her light to melt the ice that covered the rocks.

Seas and rivers began to flow, dividing the land into countries and providing water for the lush plants.

Again she returned thinking that her job was done but the Father of the Spirits asked her to make one last trip. She went again to Earth and woke the last of the sleeping spirits. Animals and birds of every type began to walk, jump, hop and crawl over every part of the world. Birds flew in the sunny skies and at last Sun Mother's work was complete.

She gathered all the creatures together and explained to them that this was their world and that they should treat it well. She asked that they live together in peace and harmony, look after each other and take care of the world that had been lovingly created for them to live in.

Then Sun Mother left Earth and made her home in the sky where she could keep watch on Earth and warm it with her rays.

Mother Nature

In this legend the Sun is called the Sun Mother because she cares for Earth in the same way as a mother provides and cares for her children. In many legends and stories around the world, Earth is called Mother Earth and all the plant and animal life on it is called Mother Nature. This is because Earth and the natural world provide us with everything we need to live – food, water, air, medicines, fuel and building materials.

Paper flowers

To make one pink flower you will need:
- pink paper 14cm x 28cm
- pencil and ruler
- scissors
- pipe cleaner
- sticky tape
- length of blue raffia

Bright asters

1   Fold the pink paper in half lengthways. Use the ruler to make pencil marks every 5mm along the unfolded edge. Now use the scissors to cut towards the fold at each pencil mark as shown.

2   Take the pipe cleaner and fold over 1cm at one end.

3   Place the pipe cleaner on the folded edge of the pink paper as shown. Roll the folded paper round and round the end of the pipe cleaner tightly.

4   Use sticky tape to tape the paper in place. Fluff out the paper petals.

5   Follow steps 1–4 to make more paper flowers. Twist the pipe cleaner stems together. Use the raffia to tie the paper flowers into a bunch.

Tissue flowers

1 Put all the strips of yellow tissue paper in a pile, lining up the edges. Fold the pile in half along its length. Make cuts 2mm apart all the way along the unfolded edge, cutting towards the fold. Stop each cut 3cm from the fold.

To make one tissue paper flower you will need:

• 2 strips of yellow tissue paper, 22cm x 10cm
• scissors and ruler
• 5 sheets of pink tissue paper, 22cm x 20cm
• pipe cleaner

2 Unfold the strips of yellow tissue paper. Lie them on top of the sheets of pink tissue paper, as shown in the photograph.

3 Starting at one end, fold over 2cm of the tissue paper stack and crease along the fold. Turn the paper stack over and fold over another 2cm of tissue paper. Keep turning and folding along the whole length of the paper. Cut a small V-shape out of each side of the folded tissue paper. Be careful not to cut all the way through the paper.

4 Twist the end of the pipe cleaner around the middle. Use scissors to round off the ends of the tissue paper.

5 Open out the folded tissue paper. Carefully separate the layers of tissue paper one at a time to create a flower.

27

Special mothers

Mothers are very special to their own children. Some women are called 'mother' because they do extraordinary things that make them special to a lot of people.

Julia Ward Howe (1819–1910)

Julia Ward Howe was an American woman who campaigned for change – for women to have the vote, for slavery to be abolished, for prisons to be improved and for world peace. This desire for peace came from knowing so many women whose sons had died in the American Civil War (1861–65). In 1870 she published her 'Mother's Day Proclamation', proposing that every year there should be a Mother's Day for Peace, so that women could work together to prevent war.

Mother Teresa (1910–97)

Mother Teresa was born in Skopje, now Macedonia. She became a nun and a missionary in India. Later she established the Missionaries of Charity, devoting her life and the work of her charity to serving the poor and the dying in Calcutta, India.

Rosa Parks (1913–2005)

In 1955, when Rosa Parks refused to give up her seat on the bus to a white man, as was expected in Montgomery, USA, at this time, she was arrested. Her actions eventually led to a change in the law, giving black and white Americans equal rights on the buses. For this and other work, she is known as the 'mother of the freedom movement'.

Templates

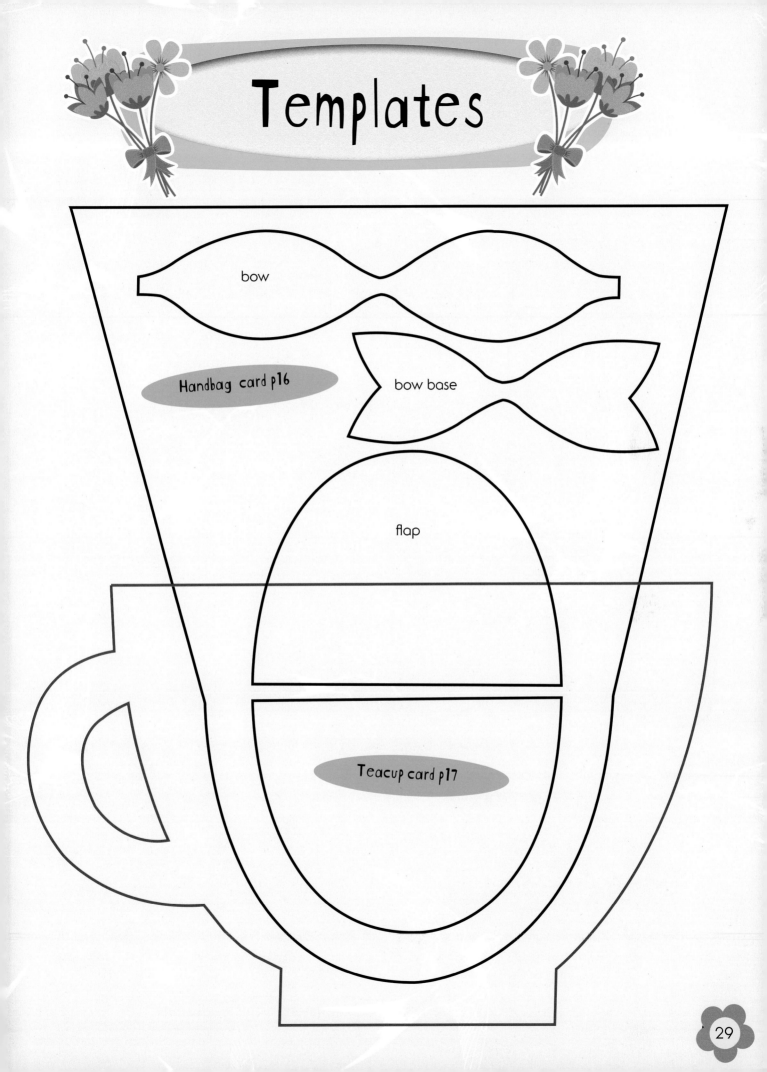

bow

Handbag card p16

bow base

flap

Teacup card p17

Coffee mug card p17

place on a fold

Mother tree p18

Indoor herb garden p22

Flower bouquet p7

bow

To make the flower bouquet card on page 7, trace and cut out:
4 large daisy shapes (1 pink, 1 orange, 1 yellow and 1 blue);
4 tulip shapes (1 pink, 1 orange, 1 yellow and 1 blue);
2 small daisy shapes (1 yellow, 1 orange);
1 background shape (green).

small daisy

large daisy

background shape

tulip

Glossary

American Civil War (1861–65) the war between the northern US states against the southern US states

apprentice someone who is taught a trade, for instance how to mend cars or make furniture, in return for working for a low wage for a number of years

brunch a late morning meal that is eaten instead of breakfast and lunch

cathedral the main church in an area – usually much bigger and grander than the other churches nearby

creation stories the stories or myths that each community or religious group tells about the beginning of the world

disciple someone who follows a religious leader. In this case, the disciples mentioned were the 12 people who were closest to Jesus

Easter Sunday the most important Christian festival when Christians celebrate Jesus Christ's resurrection (rising from the dead), three days after his crucifixion on Good Friday

equal rights when all people have the same rights – to education, pay, jobs, housing

fasting to give up eating certain foods or not eat or drink anything for a period of time

florist a shop that sells flowers

fragrant having a pleasant smell

herb any plants used to make medicine or perfume or added to food to give flavour

indigenous the people who come from a particular area. Aborigines are indigenous people in Australia

legend an old story handed down from one generation to another

Jesus Christians believe that Jesus, also called Christ, was the son of God

Lent for Christians, Lent is the 40 days that lead up to Easter Sunday (see above). Lent is a time for giving things up and many Christians do not eat a favourite food for the period of Lent

manufacturer a person or an organisation that makes things to sell to other people

missionary someone sent out on a religious mission, often to convert others to their religion

nun a woman who belongs to a religious community

posy a small bunch of flowers

retailer someone who sells goods to other people, usually from a shop

Second World War (1938–45) a war fought between the Axis Powers (Germany, Italy and Japan) against the Allies (many countries including Great Britain, France, Australia, New Zealand, India, the USA, Canada, China and the Soviet Union). Many American troops and air crews were based in Great Britain, to be closer to battles being fought in Europe

slavery when people are the property of other people

spirit some people believe that there are invisible spirits that live inside natural objects, such as trees

tradition something that has been done for a long time

vote the right to vote in elections held to elect representatives of government

Websites

www.activityvillage.co.uk/mothers-day-crafts
American website packed with ideas for
Mother's Day craft

www.bbc.co.uk/cbbc/shows/blue-peter
Click on 'Things to do' to find instructions to
make bath bombs, breakfast pancakes, an
origami heart or some tasty biscuits for your
mother on Mother's Day.

Note to parents and teachers: every effort has
been made by the Publishers to ensure that
these websites are suitable for children, that
they are of the highest educational value,
and that they contain no inappropriate or
offensive material. However, because of
the nature of the Internet, it is impossible to
guarantee that the contents of these sites will
not be altered.
We strongly advise that Internet access is
supervised by a responsible adult.

Index